SYDNEY—
where biscuits go surfing!

AIRMAIL FROM...

SYDNEY-
where biscuits go surfing!

Michael Cox

Illustrated by
Rhian Nest James

Hippo

Scholastic Children's Books,
Commonwealth House, 1-19 New Oxford Street,
London WC1A 1NU, UK

A division of Scholastic Ltd
London ~ New York ~ Toronto ~ Sydney ~ Auckland
Mexico City ~ New Delhi ~ Hong Kong

Published in the UK by Scholastic Ltd, 2000

Text copyright © Michael Cox, 2000
Illustrations copyright © Rhian Nest James, 2000

ISBN 0 439 01369 0

AIRMAIL FROM...

Sydney – where biscuits go surfing! is part of a series of books about fascinating countries around the world. Each book is made up of letters written by a boy or girl who lives in one of these countries. You might find that their English isn't always quite right (unlike yours, which is always perfect – ha ha!). So watch out for a few mistakes and crossings out. Sometimes in their letters the children use words from their own language (just like we all do!).

Although Sharon, who writes these letters, speaks English, she does use quite a lot of Australian slang words. But "no worries"! At the end of each letter she tells you the meanings of any strange words. You'll be yacking on like a real-life Ozzie before you know it!

23 September

Dear reader!

G'day and greetings from Oz! How're you doing?
My name's Sharon Beresford and I live in
Parramatta, which is in Sydney, Australia. At my
school this term we're doing a special letter-
writing project. Our class teacher, Miss Bunbury,
says that because of the
Sydney Olympics and everything,
lots of kids around the world'll
be wanting to find out tons
more about Australia. She's had
the ripper idea of letting us choose pen-pals and
write to them so's they'll know all about Oz and
what it's like to live here.

Olympic rings

OK! Here goes! I'll
start off with some info'
about me and my family.
I'm ten years old and 140
cm (4 foot 7 inches) tall.
I've got blonde hair and
brown eyes and I'm fairly
skinny. This is me!

I'm crazy about sports (especially ones you do in water!). And food! And computers! But not always in <u>that</u> order! I live with my mum, Ellen, who's a teacher, my dad, Tod, who's a sparkie, and our dog, Dennis, who's a Bitser.

My dad was born in Oz but Mum only came here from England about 15 years ago. She's still got rellies over there, including my little Pom cousin, who I've never met. I haven't got any brothers or sisters (aaah!). But I have got <u>loads</u> of mates (yeah!). They all call me Shazza, so you can too if you like! Kim, who's my best mate, is from Vietnam. She's a real sport, definitely the sort who would stick by me if ever I was in trouble. And she knows I'd do the same for her! She lives about six houses down from me and we're both in the fifth grade at our primary school in Parramatta.

My house is a bungalow and it's made out of wood and bricks with a red tiled roof. It's got a huge verandah and a really big backyard that goes all the way around it. But best of all, out back, it's got a beaut' swimming pool with a diving board. Do you have backyard swimming pools where you live? Loads of people have them here. They're just the job when you've got a big garden and stacks of hot, sunny weather.

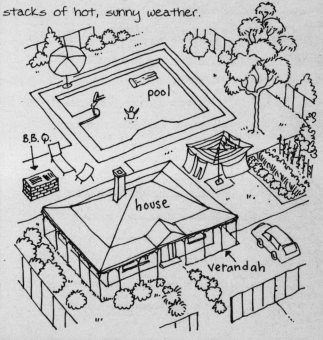

For me, having that pool in our backyard is perfect. Why? Because I'm half-girl-half-fish! Well, that's what my oldies say. They reckon I'll be sprouting a set of fins any day! I swim for the school team and also go surfing at the beach nearly every weekend. My big ambition is to swim or dive for my country in the 2008 Olympics. Every arvo, as soon as I get home from school, I put on my cozzie and do as many lengths of the pool as I can before Mum or Dad get back and tell me to get on with my homework. And that's what I'm doing right now - this letter to you! I wish all my homework was this much fun!

I think that's just about enough for my first letter, don't you? Today's a real stinker so it's time I was taking a dip in the pool.

I'll write you again in a couple of days!

Best wishes,

Shazza   your pen-pal from Parramatta

Hi again! Sorry, I'm back <u>already</u>! Mum's just had a quick squizz at my letter. She couldn't help it (she's a chalkie!). She's noticed that I've used a load of Ozzy words in it and says I should bung down their meanings for you. So, here goes:

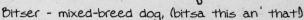

Oz - Australia

sparkie - electrician

Bitser - mixed-breed dog, (bitsa this an' that!)

rellies - relatives

Pom - English person

ripper - brilliant

sport - ace person

backyard - garden

beaut' - brilliant

oldies - what youngies sometimes call their parents

youngies - what parents sometimes call their kids

arvo - afternoon

cozzie - swimming costume

stinker - very hot day

squizz - look

chalkie - teacher

I'll write down the meanings of any more Oz words at the end of my letters. You'll be speaking Strine in no time! Oh, here's another: Strine - Australian!

25 September

Dearest pen-possum,

G'day sport, it's Shazza with the yatter from Parramatta! Waddya know about Oz? Well, even if you don't know <u>zilch</u> about Down Under, NO worries! Cos, I'll make you an Oz expert in <u>minutes</u>! Check out my globe picture:

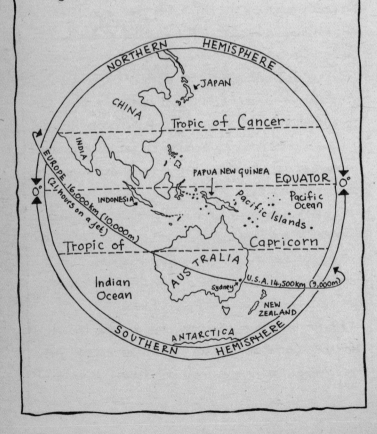

Down Under's what lots of people in Europe and the USA call Oz. Because to them we're on the other side of the earth ball. In other words, in the Southern Hemisphere. Oz was first known as Terra Australis, which means the Land in the South. Later on they settled for just calling it Australia. As well as being a country, Oz is a continent. We're the lowest and flattest of the seven continents and the only one that's all in the Southern Hemisphere. We're also the smallest

continent. But we're still really BIG! You could fit <u>all</u> of the British Isles into us <u>26</u> times! But we've only got about 18 million people. There are <u>60</u> <u>million</u> people in Britain!

Most of our people live in our cities which are all near the coast. Our great big, hot, dry centre, which we call the "outback" (or "bush") covers about two-thirds of the country and is more or less empty! As well as all that desert we've got tropical forests, tons of beaut' beaches and some mountains that get more snow than the Alps in Europe.

I'll draw you a map so you can see all the different parts of Oz, as well as our major cities and states and stuff. Look out for my house!

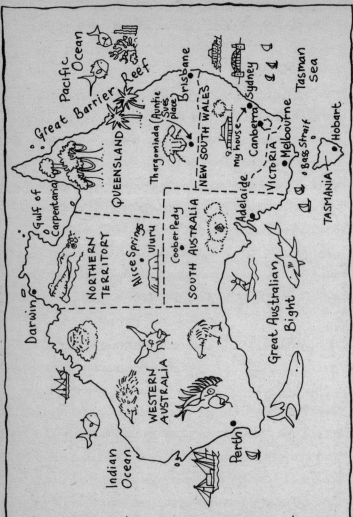

Right, now here's a question: who got to Australia first? The Europeans? Captain Cook, the famous British explorer? Nope! It was the Aborigines! Just one fact from my piccy history of Oz!

The History of Oz in a Flash!

ABOUT 50,000 YEARS AGO – The historians reckon that around this time Oz was joined to Asia by a land bridge, or that the sea was really shallow and easy to cross. So people walked (or maybe paddled?) here from Papua New Guinea. They were the ancestors of the Australian people we now call the Aborigines (original people). No one is entirely certain about this bit of our history because it happened such a long time ago.

AROUND 1600 – Sticky-beak seafarers and explorers from Europe and Asia nosed around north and west Oz but most of them thought it wasn't worth a crumpet because it was so hot and dry.

This'll never work!

It's too hot!

...and there's nothing here!

1770 – Captain James Cook sailed his ship, the Endeavour, to Tahiti in the Pacific Ocean so a load of scientists could cop a really good squizz of the planet Venus as it passed over the face of the sun. Afterwards he sailed to New Zealand and claimed it for Britain. And then he carried on west and reached the east coast of Oz. He claimed all of east Australia for Britain and called it New South Wales.

1787 – Britain was chockers with crims but had nowhere to put them! So they decided to send them as far way as possible – and you couldn't get much further away than Oz! In 1787 the Brits sent 11 boatloads of convicts here as part of an expedition called The First Fleet.

1788 – They finally landed near the place Captain Cook had named Port Jackson, and built their first settlement there. I'll tell you more about that and the convicts soon.

1790 – The Second Fleet arrived with more convicts and some supplies.

1813 – Settlers were beginning to come to Oz out of their own free choice. They thought it was a brand new country that would give them chances they never got back home in Pommyland.

1830 – By this time lots more convict settlements had been made. Altogether there were 58,000 convicts living here!

1851 - Gold was discovered in New South Wales and Victoria. Even more people came to Oz in the hope of finding their fortune!

1868 - Transportation of convicts to Oz was finally stopped. This was partly because the new free settlers in Oz weren't too keen on having boatloads of crims dumped on their doorsteps and also because good people back in Pomland had protested about transportation anyway. They said it was all horribly cruel and inhuman. Too right it was!

1901 - Oz had become six separate colonies all belonging to Britain. After Queen Victoria had told them it was OK to go ahead, the colonies joined together and became the independent Commonwealth of Australia on 1 January. Hurrah!

Hooray! Now we can manage our own affairs!

1908 - Canberra was made the capital city of Oz. (It's an aboriginal word that means meeting place)

1942– The 2nd World War was on. Darwin and Sydney were attacked by the Japanese.

1967– The Aborigines were allowed to be Australian citizens and could vote (Yes, it took that long!)

1985– Aboriginal lands started to be given back to them. About time too!

And it's only taken nearly 200 years!

1986– The film "Crocodile Dundee" came out and was a world blockbuster! You seen it?

Since 1945 lots and lots of people have come here from Europe. Did you know that Melbourne's got the third largest population of Greek people of any city in the world? Recently people've been coming from Asia too, like Kim's mum and dad.

Right! I reckon that's enough yacking on for one

day. I'm going to crash out early tonight because tomorrow me and Kim are going on a day trip with the oldies. They won't say where they're taking us, but I'm sure it'll be great!

Cop yer later, hot tomater!

S.

yatter - gossip
butchers - look
sticky-beak - nosey or inquisitive sort of person
not worth a crumpet - worthless
cop - take or see
chockers - full up
crims - criminals
Pommyland - England
yacking on - talking

By the way, did you know that some of our words come from Cockney rhyming slang? Quite a lot of the convicts came from the East End of London and brought their way of talking with them. If you take another "butcher's hook" at my word list, you'll see what I mean!

1 October

G'day pen mate!

How's you? Everything ripper in "Up Over" land? Remember that big day out I was telling you about? Well, it turned out to be even <u>better</u> than I thought it would be. We whizzed back 200 years in a time machine and got a taste of what Steak and Kidney (our nickname for Sydney) was like yonks ago. Wow! Talk about lively!

The first thing we came across as we walked down Main Street was two convicts knocking the daylights out of each other with their bare fists. Just after that we saw a gang of cons trying to escape from the prison colony by rowing a boat across the bay. They weren't free for long though. Their boat got blown out of the water by a shot from the cannon on the government boat.

Next, we

saw a convict being tried for stealing a soldier's gun! He was found guilty and ten minutes later we watched the poor bloke get hanged! Gruesome or what!

Then, just as we were deciding whether to go watch a duel or a convict being flogged, some soldiers came up and arrested my dad! They said he'd been acting suspiciously and they were putting him in the clink for at least a couple of years! We managed to get this photograph of him doing his time! Luckily he was only inside for a couple of minutes. Cos, as you've probably guessed by now, it was all

pretend! We were visiting Old Sydney, a model town, all rigged out to look like the place must have looked between 1788 and 1810. It's got old buildings and loads of people walking around dressed in old-fashioned clobber and doing the everyday things they did back then.

← me

Our day out at Old Sydney was all great fun and really entertaining but I know for sure that life in the REAL old Sydney was <u>much</u> more scary and cruddy and tough. That's because a couple of terms ago at school we did a project on how the first boat-loads of English convicts were brought to Oz and how our first settlement got started. Miss Bunbury explained to us how eighteenth century England was as rough as guts, with loads of poor people and loads of crime but hardly any room in the prisons. You could be sent to gaol or even hanged for the littlest thing. Like stealing a loaf or pinching a dress!

To get their convicts out of the way the English used to transport them to work on the plantations in America, which was a British colony at that time. But in 1776 the Americans declared their independence and threw the English out. So now they needed a fresh place to send their crims. When Captain Cook returned from Oz he told the Poms that Botany Bay would be a good spot to dump them.

So, in 1787, a total of 11 wooden sailing ships carrying 772 prisoners and about 700 sailors and soldiers set off for Oz. Just a little sea trip of 25,000 km! (15,500 miles!). The expedition was called the First Fleet and a bloke called Captain Phillip was in charge of it. Our big shock came when Miss Bunbury told us that 13 of the first prisoners sent here were <u>children</u>! They included a girl called Elizabeth Haywood and a little chimney sweep called John Hudson. He was only <u>nine</u>! Miss Bunbury said that we should pretend to be one of them and write a diary about what happened to us. Here's the one I did:

Elizabeth Haywood's Diary
by Sharon Beresford

3 May 1787.

My name is Elizabeth Haywood and I am aged 13. I was arrested for stealing a gown and a bonnet. But I didn't do it. They have put me on a sailing ship but I don't know where I am going. It is horrible. I am locked below decks with lots of thieves and murderers. The rocking of the ship and the bad smells are making me sick.

18 October 1787.

We have been at sea for three months and now we are at a place called Rio de Janeiro in a country called Brazil. A lot of the prisoners have died of sickness. Captain Phillip has decided that we should stop for supplies and rest. We are being given oranges to eat to make us all well again.

20 January 1788.

We have been sailing for eight months altogether but now we have arrived in a strange land at a place they call Botany Bay. They say that Captain Phillip does not like it because there is no fresh water or shade. So we are sailing on.

27 January 1788.

We sailed up the coast to a big piece of water with land on three sides of it. Captain Phillip has said we will stay here. He has named it Sydney Cove after Viscount Sydney who is an important man in the government back in London.

They have stuck a British flag in the soil.

20 February 1788.

It is very, very sunny here every day and the sky is always blue. I have never been this hot before in my whole life. Everyone is busy building huts from mud and sticks. I have been set to work with the women making wooden pegs to hold the roof tiles on. I am used to this sort of work because back in England I was a clog maker.

26 February 1788.

While we were collecting the peg wood today I spotted some people watching us from the bushes. Their skin was black all over and they had hardly any clothes on. I have also seen many bright-coloured birds and some animals that look like little dragons. This is the strangest place I have ever been. It has got lots of big rocks and odd-looking flowers and trees all over everywhere.

26 February 1788.

Today I heard one of the women say that some prisoners who escaped got killed by the black people. But I think that it was more likely the men who guard us what did it. They are very, very cruel! Yesterday I saw them whip a man until he had no skin left on his back just because he wanted a moment's rest from his work. I am frightened and I want to go home. But I do not think I will ever see England again. *Elizabeth*

I wonder what really happened to Elizabeth? Anyway, that settlement she was helping build grew into the massive city of three-and-a-half million people that I live in today. In my next letter I'll tell you just what it's like nowadays!

Shazza

yonks - a long time
cruddy - tatty
rough as guts - very rough and rowdy

Hiyah pen-mate!

How y'doin'? Here in Parramatta, the sun's shining, the kookaburras are laughing and the barbies are smokin'!

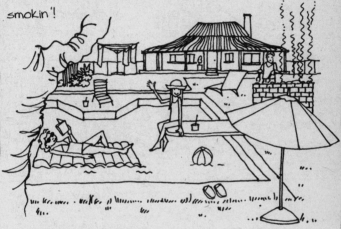

There weren't any flies on ol' Captain Phillip, were there?! He must have been a really smart bloke to have spotted that Sydney Cove was such a beaut' place for a settlement! Most Sydneysiders agree with him. They say that Steak and Kidney is the "best address on earth". As such, I reckon it's time you had a gander at our great city. I can't take you everywhere so I've drawn you this bird's eye squizz of our biggest and best - all to give you...

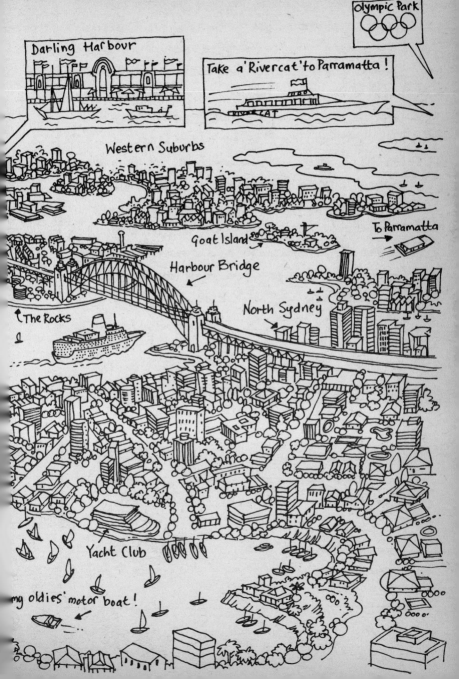

1. <u>Parramatta</u> - This is where I live. It's about 20 clicks from the centre of Sydney, but I thought I'd make it the first stop before you whizz around S and K proper! Parramatta is an Aborigine word which means "the place where the eels sleep" - so you won't be surprised to learn that it's right next to the Parramatta River.

Captain Phillip and his mates built the first ever farm in Oz here, back in the days when they were looking for somewhere to grow some decent grub for them and the convicts. But it's not a farm any more! It's a mass of roads and houses and schools and backyards and stuff! More than 130,000 people live here now and the whole place has sort of got joined on to the main bit of Sydney.

2. <u>Sydney Harbour</u> - This is the biggest natural harbour in the world! There's always loads of boats in it, including my oldies' little motor launch (which I love going for trips around the bay in!). Cos there's always plenty to see, as you can see!

I like it best when they start the Sydney to Hobart Yacht Race from here on Boxing Day.

3. <u>Fort Denison</u> - In the old days the extra bad convicts were stuck out here and put on a diet

of bread and water. That's why it's also called Pinchgut Island!

4. <u>Sydney Cove</u> - This is the place that Captain Phillip chose to build the first houses.

5. <u>Bennelong Point</u> - This is named after an Aborigine who was Captain Phillip's servant when he became Governor of Sydney. He made him wear European clothes and later on he took him to England to show him off to all his posh

Pom mates. Bennelong wasn't too happy about this and when he came back to Oz he ran away. Some people say that not long afterwards he fell out with his tribe, then burned himself to death on this very spot!

6. <u>The Opera House</u> - My dad reckons this is one of the seven modern wonders of the world. What do you think to those wacky roofs? They reckon the architect got the idea while he was peeling an orange! They remind lots of people of ships' sails. But they make me think of sharks' fins! Ooo-er!

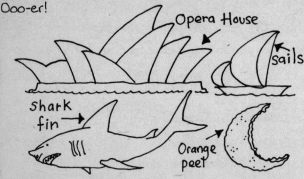

Opera House

sails

Shark fin

Orange peel

7. <u>Sydney Harbour Bridge</u> - This was opened in 1932, took nine years to build, 16 workmen got killed doing it and the city only finished paying for it in 1988! With its eight lanes for traffic, a double-track railway, a footpath and a cycleway, it's got the widest deck of any bridge in the

world. But it <u>still</u> gets traffic jams (so use the new tunnel, like we often do!). Sydneysiders call it the Coathanger! Guess why!

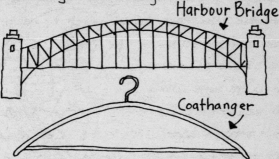

Harbour Bridge

Coathanger

8. <u>The Monorail</u> - A lot of people call this the "monster rail". They don't like it cos it's so futuristic looking. But I think it's ace! Like something out of a science fiction movie. It thunders around on its overhead track and you get great views of the harbour and city. Don't miss it!

9. <u>Sydney Tower</u> - Sydney's tallest building at 305 metres. Gives you really spectacular views of the city. Every year a bunch of keep-fit freaks have a race up its 1,474 stairs.

only 1,466 to go!

I reckon that should be enough to keep you busy. You'll love Sydney! There's so much happening all the time. Street clowns and jugglers, buskers, skateboarders, people sitting at the pavement cafes ... everyone having fun in the sun! And I <u>still</u> haven't told you about the beaut' beaches - I'll save <u>them</u> for another

letter! It's amazing to think that all this has grown out of that mud hut settlement in just over 200 years! I wonder what Governor Phillip would think if he could see it all now? Maybe he'd be gagging for a spin on the monster rail?

Check ya later,

Shazza

barbie - barbecue
a gander at - a look at
clicks - kilometres

5 November

Dear pen-mate from Up Over,

Hi pal! How's y'doin' and what's your weather like o.s.? You gettin' a monsoon, or a blizzard or a heat wave ... or just one of those miserable, cold, grey days like Mum says they're always getting in Pomland? Here in Sydney it's fining up now because our summer's almost here. Our seasons are topsy-turvy to the ones in the Northern Hemisphere. So when people in Up Over are getting winter we're having summer! I've drawn you this calendar so's you'll know what happens when.

New South Wales seasons →

Being such a huge continent our weather and seasons are different for different parts. Our north is tropical with just a wet and a dry season while our south has mild winters and hot summers a bit like they get around the Mediterranean area of Europe. Oz weather is absolutely brilliant if you're like me and enjoy being outdoors a lot. But sometimes it misbehaves and causes <u>BIG</u> problems. As you'll find out when you read...

The FerOZity Forecast
OZ's Freaky Forces of Nature

HEAT – Australia's a world record breaker for heat. In Western Australia in 1889 the thermometer stayed above 37°C (99°F) for a brain-sizzling 160 days! You didn't need a pan and cooker to fry your cackleberries. You just dropped them on the rocks!

Our highest ever recorded temperature was a scorching 53.1°C (127.6°F) in Queensland in 1889. When the famous explorer Charles Sturt got stuck in the central desert in 1844 it was so hot that it melted the lead in his pencils and stopped his hair growing. Saved him a fortune in writing-paper and razor blades! Luckily he was camped next to a waterhole so he managed to survive the heat and make it back to civilization when things cooled off a bit.

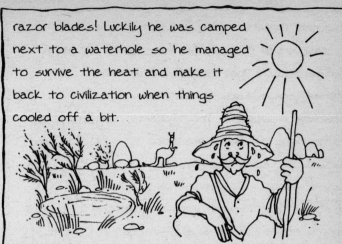

DROUGHT – About one-third of Australia is desert so we get lots of times when it doesn't rain at all for months, or even years! So they don't sell a lot of stormsticks in the outback! Here's a story my dad told me about a place called Curtin Springs:

They had a drought that lasted ten years. No rain at all. As such, there was a ten-year-old boy living there who had never ever seen rain in his whole life! When the rain finally came, the poor kid was so scared by it that he completely freaked out and fainted! He only came to when

his dad threw a bucket of bulldust over him!

Lakes and rivers in Oz are forever drying up. So we've even got fish who've learned to bury themselves in the mud when this happens. They survive by staying put until their pond decides to come back again!

dum de dum

BUSH FIRES – What with the heat and dryness, bush fires are a really _BIG_ danger in Oz. In 1939 almost the whole state of Victoria caught fire. In 1994 bush fires burned a massive area of grass and trees and destroyed 100 homes in New South Wales. They came within just a few kilometres of central Sydney. The Opera House was covered with hot ash! The fires are often fanned by roaring hot winds and race along even faster than a car travelling at top speed! And they can jump across wide valleys!

Lots of Australian trees and plants actually like fire! They seem to go out of their way to encourage it by dumping bark and leaves on the ground. Straight after the fire it looks like they've been wiped out but a few months later the burned trees get their leaves back and bushes have regrown. A lot of the trees have buds under their bark all ready and waiting to spring into action as soon as it's been burned away by fire. And the fruits of other plants actually need the fire's heat to help them burst open and spread their seeds!

It's not so good for the animals though. Some escape by burrowing underground to hide from the flames but others just get burned up.

FLOODS – Floods often come after a big dry. And when they do it happens <u>fast</u>! Here's a tip: don't ever camp on a dried up creek bed! There could be a rain storm going on 200 kilometres upstream. Then you might find yourself being suddenly swept away like a rat down a drain pipe.

The big rains often wash all the top soil away but they have good effects too. When it rains in the outback after a long drought it sometimes makes billions of seeds explode into life. In no time at all the desert is covered by a blanket of brilliant colour! When this happens in Western Australia, the Aborigines call the carpet of blue flowers that suddenly appears, the "floor of the sky".

CYCLONES – These are really strong winds that whirl around and around and cause all sorts of chaos. One of our worst ever ones was called Cyclone Tracy. When it hit the northern Australian city of Darwin on Christmas Day 1974 it blew cars into the air and lifted the roofs right off houses. Scareeey!

In just four hours, more than two-thirds of Darwin's buildings had been flattened completely and the rest were really badly damaged. What a Chrissie present! No one knows how fast Tracy's winds were because they smashed the wind-measuring machine at the airport when they reached 440 km per hour! Sadly, 66 people were also killed by Tracy and lots more got injured.

Interesting fact for you! In the northern hemisphere, cyclone winds whirl in an anti-clockwise direction and in the southern hemisphere they go clockwise. Though I'm sure if I ever got caught in one I wouldn't hang around to check this out!

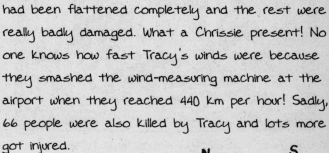

Now for a news update on the adventures of Shazza. Last night me and Kim and my oldies went out for a slap-up meal. Guess where to?

Only to the new Vietnamese restaurant which Kim's mum and dad have just opened in the shopping mall down the road. It was ace!

Everyone really enjoyed the meal ... apart from Grandpa. I think he would have preferred boiled beef and spuds any day. Right! Sun's out and we're headed for the beach this arvo so I'll be signing off! Stay cool, sport!

Shazza

o.s. - overseas
Pomland - England
cackleberries - hens' eggs
stormsticks - umbrellas
bulldust - the dust you find all over the outback

12 November

Hi mate,

It's Shazza here. Are you ready for the latest Paramatta natter? Last weekend we had a party for Grandpa's birthday, and we all ended up having a butchers at the family photo album and talking

about the old days here. Grandpa said that the main reason us Beresfords are in Oz today is because <u>his</u> great, great, great grandpa picked some bloke's pocket in a market-place in

England in the early 1800s, then got caught and sent here in one of those wooden sailing ships I told you about.

I don't suppose my way way back grandpop felt out of place when he arrived here. Around then, eight out of every ten people in Oz were criminals. Not surprising, when you think the Poms were shipping 'em here by the boatload. Most of the convicts were sent here for seven, 14 or 21 years, then given their freedom. Afterwards, rather than going back to Pomland, they'd usually get a bit of land and settle down to farming or something.

Not all of them gave up crime. All the gold that more honest blokes were digging up was just too tempting for some of 'em. Crims known as bushrangers wandered around robbing stage coaches and banks. They had crazy names like Captain Moonlight, Captain Thunderbolt and Mad Dog Morgan. The most famous one was Ned Kelly. Lots of people reckoned he was the Ozzy Robin Hood. It was said that after he'd robbed a bank the local poor people would all pay their bills with new pound notes! Guess why! Here's Ned's story for you - it's a ripper yarn.

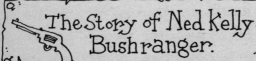

The Story of Ned Kelly - Bushranger.

In the old days of Oz there lived a boy called Ned Kelly. He was the eldest of eight kids and a hard working lad. He once saved a boy from drowning and was awarded a green sash (ribbon) which he treasured all his life. When he was 11, his dad died, and Ned had to become the man of the family. It was around this time that he began his life of crime by becoming a

horse thief. When Ned was caught one time his mum tried to clobber the policeman with a shovel, and she was sent to prison for three years!

Ned and his brother, Dan, vowed to avenge their mum's arrest, and they formed a gang and hid out in the hills. While they were hiding they ambushed and shot dead three policemen at

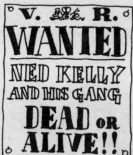

Stringybark Creek. A reward of £1,000 was offered for finding Ned, and the biggest man-hunt in Australia's history was organized.

But the gang stayed free and went in for capturing whole towns and holding them hostage! They'd lock the policemen in the jail and keep the townsfolk prisoners as they partied with them all weekend. People began to think of them as heroes.

Then one day Ned and the gang took over a town and held all the people hostage in a pub. They planned to lure a train-load of cops to town and then derail the train. But while Ned was drunk he told the local chalkie about his plan and the teacher managed to escape and stop the train. The cops got Ned and his gang trapped inside the pub and there was a terrific shoot-out.

All the gang got killed even though they were wearing bullet-proof armour they'd had made from metal plough blades. Ned got shot in the legs and taken prisoner and when they took off his armour they saw that he was still wearing his treasured green sash!

He was sentenced to death. 3,200 people signed a petition against his execution and 5,000 people came to see his hanging. Just before he died, Ned mumbled, "Such is life!" He was only 25 years old!

Actually, I think that over the years people have changed this story and

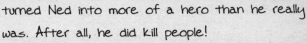

turned Ned into more of a hero than he really was. After all, he did kill people!

By the way if you're wondering about those pound notes Ned gave away, we got rid of our pounds, shillings and pence in 1966 and went over to Australian dollars and cents.

Right! I've got to stop scribbling now. I'm meeting Kim in two ticks. Me and her are robbing our local post office at two o'clock sharp this arvo!

See yah,

S.

The Parramatta Gang!

PS Not all Ozzies are descended from convicts. My Auntie Jean (that's dad's sister-in-law) comes from Adelaide in South Australia. Her ancestors came here of their own free will, like lots of people who settled in that part of Oz. Just for a joke, Auntie Jean likes to call us Sydney people "chain rattlers" (yeah, guess why!). Nobody minds though. All that transportation stuff was far too long ago to get upset about!

19 November

G'day sport,

Now that you know a bit about Sydney I think it's time you had a bo-peep at some other really bonzer bits of Oz. I'm sure you'll get here for your hols sooner or later. Maybe you've even got some rellies here who you'll visit one day? Just so's you know all about our biggest and bestest, I've made you a walkabout guide.

Walkabout means a wander around. It's an Australian Aborigine idea. They just up sticks and take off where ever their fancy leads them, checking out the scene as they go. But don't <u>you</u> do that! Just do your walking about when you actually <u>get</u> to the places. Like with loads of spots in Oz the

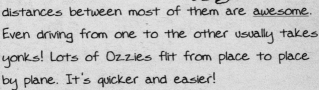

distances between most of them are <u>awesome</u>. Even driving from one to the other usually takes yonks! Lots of Ozzies flit from place to place by plane. It's quicker and easier!

SHAZZA'S GREAT

① The Great Barrier Reef

<u>What is it?</u> - It's the largest coral reef in the world. You can even see it from space! Also, it's the largest structure on earth built by living creatures. Coral reefs are made from lots of living stalks called polyps. When the polyps die they leave a shell. More polyps grow on the little skellies. So the reef just carries on getting bigger and bigger!

← polyps' eggs

← polyps

Great Sandy Desert

② Uluru

④ Coober Pedy

③ Rottnest Island

Nullarbor Plain

The Great Barrier reef is actually made of thousands of coral reefs and islands joined

OZ WALKABOUT

together. They reach 250 metres up from the ocean floor in some parts. People are very worried about the reef at the moment cos it's getting messed up by pollution and tourists. They've made it a World Heritage Site to try and protect it from greedy-guts businessmen who want to build hundreds of new holiday resorts right next to it!

Coral is also the favourite tucker of hungry sea creatures called crown-of-thorns starfish who're munching their way through great chunks of it.

<u>Where is it?</u> - In the sea all along the north eastern coast of Australia. It stretches all the way from Central Queensland to Western Papua in

(map labels:) ① Great Barrier Reef · Great Dividing Range · Stony Desert · Sydney

New Guinea. That's the distance from London to Rome in Italy!

London
Rome

Great Barrier Reef

<u>What to do</u> - 2,000 types of amazing fish live around the reef so it's brilliant for scuba-diving and snorkelling. Or just check out the under-sea world through the glass bottom of a boat - it's out of this, er ... world?

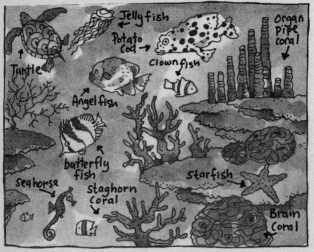

Jellyfish
Potato Cod
Organ Pipe Coral
Clownfish
Turtle
Angel fish
butterfly fish
Seahorse
Staghorn Coral
Starfish
Brain Coral

<u>Whoops!</u> - Captain Cook's ship got stuck on the Barrier Reef. To get it floating again the crew

chucked loads of stuff overboard. They even bunged a cannon in the water. It was fished out later - then bunged in our National Library at Canberra.

② Uluru

<u>What is it?</u> - Some people say it's the greatest stone on earth but it's actually the tip of a massive bed of pebbles that lay on the bed of an inland sea about 600 million years ago! Most of it's hidden under the ground but the bit sticking up is gob-smackingly <u>gi-normous</u>! It used to be called Ayers Rock after some big-noise Ozzy politician, but Uluru, which means Big

Pebble, is its proper Aboriginal name. It's a very special and sacred place for the Aborigines and was given back to them in 1985.

<u>Where is it?</u> - In the middle of the desert, 1,395 km (865 miles) south of Darwin in our Northern Territory.

<u>What to do</u> - You can climb it, but people don't really like you to do this, as it is a sacred place for the Aborigines. There's chain to haul yourself up on, but be careful! If you do happen to fall you'll be in big trouble - Uluru's 348m (1,142 feet) high! If you've not got a head for heights walk around the base and check out the caves and Aboriginal rock paintings. It's 9.4 km (5.9 miles) all the way round so it'll take you between three and four hours!

<u>Wow!</u> - The rock changes colour during the day. Mostly it's a dullish grey colour but in the mornings and evenings it glows brilliant orangey red. That's because the low sun picks out the iron in the rock which rain water has turned rusty.

③ Rottnest Island

<u>What is it?</u> - It's a paradise island with beaut' white beaches. It's 11 clicks wide and five clicks long and surrounded by clear blue water. Ozzies all call it Rotto. Cars aren't allowed on it so's you have to walk or cycle everywhere. That's right! It's safe and peaceful <u>and</u> unpolluted!

<u>Where is it?</u> - Off the coast of Fremantle in Western Australia.

<u>What to do</u> - Get a load of the local fish and chips. Cruise around Rotto in a glass-bottom boat and take a bo-peep at the sea life and the shipwrecks on the seabed.

<u>Well I never!</u> - When a sticky-beak Dutch explorer was having a butchers at it in 1796 he freaked out when he saw that the whole place appeared to be crawling with giant rats. So he called it Rottnest! (Dutch for Rats' Nest.) But, he was wrong! They weren't rats! They were quokkas. They're marsupials, about the size of hares. And <u>much</u> nicer than rats!

Aah! Rotten rats on the rampage!

By the way, marsupials are mammals like kangaroos and possums who live in a pouch on their mum's body while they're growing.

④ Coober Pedy

<u>What is it?</u> - It's a mining town in the outback where they dig for precious gems called opals. The

opal!

first one was found there by a teenage boy back in 1915. Forty different nationalities of people have been digging there ever since! Even though opals are supposed to bring bad luck!

<u>Where is it?</u> - In the Outback - 553 km north of Port Augusta.

<u>What to do</u> - Stay in the underground hotel! Then visit the underground shops and churches. Also, check out Crocodile Harry's place. He's a retired crocodile hunter who grows vegetables in the wrecked cars just outside his burrow.

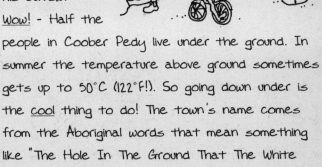

<u>Wow!</u> - Half the people in Coober Pedy live under the ground. In summer the temperature above ground sometimes gets up to 50°C (122°F!). So going down under is the <u>cool</u> thing to do! The town's name comes from the Aboriginal words that mean something like "The Hole In The Ground That The White Blokes Live In".

<u>Watch out!</u> - There are a quarter of a million old mine shafts around C.P. which are a) real <u>hard</u> to see and b) real <u>easy</u> to fall down!

   OK! Now to <u>my</u> travel news! Last night my dad was on the blower yacking away ten-to-the-dozen with his sister, my Auntie Sue, who's got a sheep station in Queensland. All the time he kept looking at me and grinning and nodding. When he finally put down the rap rod he asked me if I wanted to go and stay at Sue's place in the summer hollies. I said, "Too right I do!" So it looks like I'm gonna be a junior jilleroo for a while. Way to go, mate!

Best wishes,

Shazza

Baa!

bonzer - great
a bo-peep - a look
skellies - skeletons
tucker - food
blower - telephone
rap rod - telephone
jilleroo - a girl who works on a sheep station

24 November

G'day mate!

How's things with you? I aren't half looking forward to spending January at Sue's sheep station. It'll be bonzer! Not everyone in Oz gets to visit the outback so it feels like I'm going on a <u>really</u> big adventure. It'll be nice to get away from all the people and traffic and stuff in Paramatta for a while. I'll be flying to Thargomindah where Sue will meet me in her beaut' ute - a 4WD! After that she'll drive me 250 km through the bush to her place.

I suppose if I'd been living in Oz about 200 years ago it would have felt like an even bigger adventure! They didn't even have proper maps! The first Europeans in Oz all settled near the coast where it was fairly safe and not <u>too</u> hot with fresh water and grass for the animals. So, what lay "back o' beyond" was <u>anyone's guess</u>! Many people thought that there was a huge sea in the middle of Australia. And some of the convicts reckoned that if they escaped and crossed the big mountains behind Sydney they'd be in China straight away! S'right! Their geography wasn't too hot!

The ginormous, unknown, central part of Australia got to be a big temptation for a load of adventurous sticky-beaks. All sorts of blokes who were really brave (or maybe a grape short of a bunch?) decided they'd go walkabout and take a look see what was "beyond the black stump". So they set off on exploring expeditions. Quite a few had to give up very quickly because of things like swarms of blood-sucking flies, brain-roasting heat, starvation, illness, drought or attacks by Aborigines. And some never made it back at all!

Two of the most famous Australian explorers were Robert Burke and William Wills. Their big idea was to be the first Europeans to get all the way from Melbourne on the south coast of Oz to the Gulf of Carpentaria on the north coast ... then all the way back again!

Just a gentle stroll of 2,413 kilometres (1,500 miles) each way! I've made you this picture-story so you can see how they <u>almost</u> made it – but were beaten by some really rotten luck on their last lap!

The Sad Story of Burke + Wills

In 1860 Burke and Wills set off from Melbourne with a bunch of mates, loads of horses and camels and 20 tons of supplies. Thousands of cheering people gave them a hero's send off, with Burke proudly leading the expedition on his grey charger, Billy. They even had uniforms specially made for the trip.

Burke was in a real hurry to get to the coast so after a while he made a base camp at a place called Cooper's Creek. He left most of the men and provisions there while just him and Wills and two other blokes called King and Gray carried on.

They finally reached the sea but as soon as they did they had to start back again cos they were worried that their tucker would run out.

Their return journey was terrible. The heat was scorching and the supplies soon ran short. They had to kill and eat their horses and camels – even Billy! Gray got sick and died. Some people reckon that Burke beat him to death for stealing extra food, but no one knows for sure!

That's gratitude for you!

The guys at Cooper's Creek base camp waited a whole extra month for Burke to return but in the end they'd had enough. Before they left they buried some supplies next to a tree then carved the word "DIG" into its trunk so Burke'd know where to find the tucker.

Guess what! Just hours after they'd gone, Burke and the others turned up. And here's where it gets <u>really</u> unlucky! They decided to move on again. So they wrote a letter to say where they were headed, buried it by the tree, and set off. But for some reason they <u>didn't</u> change the sign on the tree! Maybe they weren't thinking right cos of being so hungry? That happens to me!

Moving on. What a scorcher! Hope to see you alive! Love Burke and Wills.

Not long afterwards the rescue party returned to the DIG tree. But, seeing that nothing had changed, they thought that Burke hadn't made it back from the coast so they didn't go looking for him. And all the time he was just a few miles away!

66

Not long afterwards Burke and Wills starved to death. Their mate John King was luckier. He was found by some Aborigine people who fed him and looked after him until he was rescued.

What a story! I suppose nowadays that sort of expedition would have a TV crew filming it every minute of the way! You can still see the "DIG" tree at Cooper's Creek but the message has been cemented over to stop the tree from dying.

So now you can see why almost nine out of ten Australians still live in the big cities near the coast today. It's only little Aussie battlers like Auntie Sue who brave the outback!

Speak to you soon,

Shazza

ute - 4 wheel drive vehicle, like a Jeep or Landrover
back o' beyond - middle of nowhere
beyond the black stump - the outback
a grape short of a bunch - mad

29 December

Dear readeroo,

How're you? It's Shazza with some hot chatter from Paramatta! First off, Merry Chrissie to you! You enjoyin' your hols? Gettin' any snow or anything? It's 25°C here in Sydney, so, as usual, we've been spending most of our hol' by the pool or on the beach. On Chrissie day Kim and her folks came round to our place and we all had traditional Pommy Christmas dinner with roast turkey and spuds and all the trimmings! But outside it was almost hot enough for the turkey to roast all on its own!

The old-fashioned Christmas dinner was a special treat for Grandpa because he likes <u>his</u> tucker traditional. He's not like the younger people here who go for all different sorts of food. Guess what Grandpa's favourite food is! Meat pie floater! Now <u>that's</u> a real Ozzie special! It's a meat pie floating in pea soup. You fancy it? Grandpa likes his with at least a couple of buckets of tomato sauce dolloped on. I think it's

gross! His other favourite thing
is Vegemite sangers! Uuurgh!
Anyway, I reckon Kim and her
folks were right tickled with
the roast turkey. But somehow I
don't think it'll be going on the menu at their
restaurant!

On Boxing Day we went to Sydney Harbour and
saw the Yacht Race set off for Hobart in
Tasmania, Oz's island state. The boats are always
escorted out to sea by a fleet of pleasure
boats. Including ours! What a fantastic sight it is!

I just hope nothing goes wrong for the sailors.
The other year massive storms hit the race and
some were drowned! I've drawn you their route:

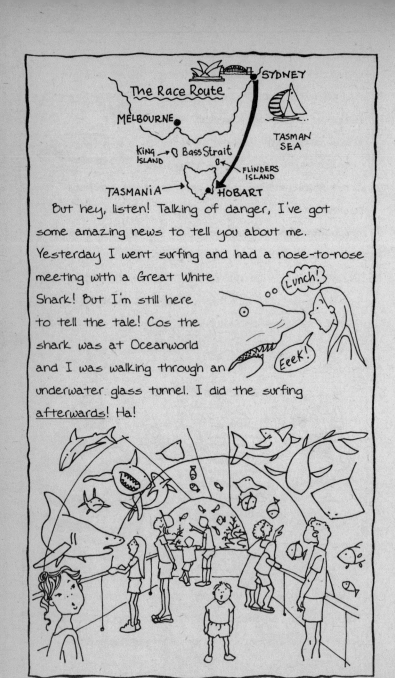

The Race Route

SYDNEY

MELBOURNE

TASMAN SEA

KING ISLAND → Bass Strait

FLINDERS ISLAND

TASMANIA → HOBART

But hey, listen! Talking of danger, I've got some amazing news to tell you about me. Yesterday I went surfing and had a nose-to-nose meeting with a Great White Shark! But I'm still here to tell the tale! Cos the shark was at Oceanworld and I was walking through an underwater glass tunnel. I did the surfing afterwards! Ha!

Lunch!

Eeek!

Oceanworld is at Manly where we were having a day out with Kim and her folks. "Seven miles from Sydney and a thousand miles from care" is what they say about Manly! It's got the lot: a great surfing beach, a funfair and the Oceanworld aquarium where you can watch a diver swimming with the sharks!

Guess why it's called Manly! When Governor Phillip first sailed into the harbour he spotted some tough-looking Aborigine blokes and said that they looked "manly". And the name stuck! Hey! If those Aborigines had been weedy wimps maybe Manly would now be called Wussy?

71

Manly Beach is my second fave after Palm Beach, which is bit further north. If you watch the Aussie soap, "Home and Away", you'll know that one for sure. It's the one you see at the beginning, 'cept on TV they call it Summer Bay. The other beach you may have heard of is Bondi. That's the really famous one where they hold a huge party on Christmas day. Its name comes from Boondi, which was what the Aborigines called it. They named it after the booming sound the waves make as they crash on to the shore.

Altogether we've got 34 brilliant surfing beaches around Sydney. But, can you believe this? Until about 100 years ago sea bathing in the daylight was banned here cos people weren't supposed to be seen wandering around in their reginalds! Then, in 1902, a bloke broke the law by going for a daytime swim on Manly Beach!

After that everyone started doing it and nowadays we go to the beach all the time! Late in the arvo you'll even see people in the sea and families chilling out on the sand long after dark.

I go to the beach whenever I can because I'm a waxhead. I've been surfing since I was four. I even go surfing in the winter, when I wear my wet suit to keep warm. I've been to surf school and learned mouth to mouth revival technique and water safety as well as some really nifty surfing moves. I'm definitely no shark biscuit but I still

come off my board. That's why I have it tied to my ankle by a tether-rope so's I don't loose it!

Sometimes the sea can be dangerous. There's currents and rips and stuff that can carry you

miles out really quickly. Rips are a sort of tide.
You have to keep an eye on the flags. Here's
what the different ones mean:

Red — It's safe to bathe between these.

Amber — The surf is dangerous. Not a good idea to swim.

Red — Beach closed. Very dangerous for bathing.

Siren — Get out of the water FAST! — Probably sharks, stingers or freak waves!

   Listen! If you do get
caught by a rip, stay calm
and float on your back with
one arm in the air. That
way the surf lifesaver'll
know you're in trouble and
come to your rescue. You'll
recognize the lifesavers by

their red and yellow hats. The Sydney ones've been life-saving ever since the early 1900s and have done more than 400,000 rescues!

Back in 1938, on what's now known as Black Sunday, a ginormous avalanche of freak waves hit Bondi beach. In no time at all, hundreds of people were swept out to sea but, because of the skill of 60 brave surf-lifesavers, all but six were rescued!

My other fave activities are rollerblading and skateboarding. Both are a bit like surfing on land! So to finish here's two piccies of my favourite bits of kit:

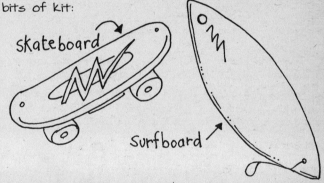

skateboard

Surfboard

Now you can see why I'm always on a board but never bored! Ha! See yah!

Best wishes,

Shazza

PS I don't do nearly as much surfing in the winter as I do in the summer. Winter's when I spend some time doing the other sort of

surfing ... on my computer! Or I go on the internet and e-mail my cousins in Adelaide. And when I'm not doing that I watch TV or take Dennis for a walk around Parramatta.

me and my computer

Vegemite - brown sandwich spread made from yeast

sangers - sandwiches

wussy - weak or wimpish

reginalds - undies (rhymes with Grundies - Reg Grundy is a big noise in Oz TV. Check out our soaps for his name in the credits)

waxhead - surfing nut

shark biscuit - beginner surfer

stingers - stinging jellyfish

Yum Yum!

30 December

G'day mate!

How's you? OK, I hope! I reckon that I'm dead lucky to be writing you this letter today! Rather than just <u>dead</u>. Yesterday, I thought I'd had my chips! This is what happened. Mum said I should strike a blow for my pocket money so I was sorting out the bucket and stuff ready to wash our car when I picked up this damp cloth. There, looking mean as a cut snake and eyeballing me from the middle of it, was a <u>funnel web</u>!

I s'pose I better explain what that is. It just happens to be the most dangerous, bad-tempered and deadly spider in the whole world. This one looked mad as a maggot and was rearing up on its back legs all fired up to go the knuckle with me (as they all do!). Like something from a horror movie!

Being a trainee coward I screamed and froze. That was when Mum came in. The moment she saw the funnel web she grabbed a tin of car polish and clobbered it hard. And that was that. One dead beastie! I hate to think what would have happened if I'd not spotted it.

There are quite a few different kinds of nasties to beware of in Oz. So, just to make you <u>completely</u> terrified of <u>ever</u> coming here I've made you a list of Australia's most unwanted. Only kidding. None of these nasties are that common. And if you take a few precautions you'll have nothing to worry about. I've given each of the nuisances on the list a "skull-and-cross-bones" danger rating. Hey! I've just noticed that they nearly all begin with the letter "s"! Spookeee!

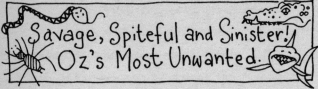

Savage, Spiteful and Sinister! Oz's Most Unwanted.

SHARKS – There are more recorded shark attacks in Oz than anywhere else in the world. That doesn't mean to say we actually <u>get</u> more! Maybe Australians keep better records of attacks and write down every single

one whilst people in other places aren't so bothered? Nowadays, I think, about one unlucky person gets killed by an after dark about once a year. (Bet the poor bloke's getting a bit fed up, whoever he is!)

There are all sorts of things to protect us from sharks so it's fairly safe to swim in the sea. While you're having fun there are shark lookout patrols watching out for the guys with the big teeth. There are shark nets in the water as well to stop them getting too close to the beaches.

SUN - There are hardly any days when we don't get sunshine in Sydney, same as lots of places in Oz! Problem is, Oz is really near to that dirty great hole in the ozone layer that the scientists are always telling us about. The one that lets the sun's harmful rays through. It's over the South Pole and sometimes it sort of wanders our way! What with us Ozzies being mad on outdoor stuff and sunbaking we have to be very careful. Otherwise we end up with skin cancer!

79

Most people follow the government "Slip Slop Slap" code! Before you get too much sun, you:

Slip on your T shirt   **Slop** on some Sun block   **Slap** on your hat!

And bang on your sunnies too! The bright sunlight can do terrible things to your eyes! The other thing too much sun will give you is sunstroke! I got it once and felt crook for days!

SNAKES – We've got some really mean snakes in Oz. Like taipans, tigers and sea snakes, to name but a few! The worst is the taipan. Did you know that one taipan

is said to carry enough poison to kill 200,000 mice! Somehow, I don't think the mice would ever try putting this to the test!

SPIDERS – You already know a bit about our funnel webs: the most poisonous spider in the world. And only found in Steak and Kidney. What have we done to deserve them? They're black and chunky little beasts named after their cone-shaped webs. You can die from their bite. If you do get bitten, go straight to hospital where the bite will be treated just like a snake bite.

The other spider to watch out for is the redback, especially when you go to the dunny! They like to hang around under the seat. They're tiny and black with red patches on their back. The males are supposed to be the dangerous ones. But I can't tell one from the other!

SEA WASPS –
also known as
box jellyfish or
stingers. They're
almost invisible
and their sting
can kill you. Their

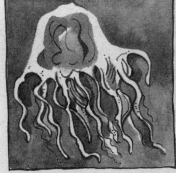

southern cousins, bluebottles, have a very painful sting, but nobody dies from them. Their stinging tentacles can stretch two metres away from their body! If they get you, put vinegar on the stings. The lifeguards often have it ready and waiting on beaches. The stinger season is May to October.

freshie

saltie

SALTIES AND FRESHIES -

Not snacks! Crocs! Fancy yourself as Crocodile Dundee? Well, get up to our Northern Territories. Up there we've got two sorts of croc: freshwater and saltwater. The smaller freshies are supposed to be less dangerous, though I wouldn't tangle with one! But it's the big salties which can grow up to six metres long (my dad, end to end, times three!) that are really dangerous. They don't even seem to know they're salties. Instead of sticking to saltwater river mouths they get everywhere! So look before you leap! There might well be one lurking in that swimming pool or pond that you might be about to dive into one sweltering, summer afternoon.

Watch for the warning signs, too. Would you believe that some really stupid tourists steal them for souvenirs? What drongos!

Salties, who're also known as snapping logs, can move really fast on land. They sometimes catch people or animals who're standing too near the water's edge. They shoot out of the water like a missile from a submarine then use their tail to drag their victim under water.

Well, don't say I haven't warned you! Seriously

though, don't worry too much about all this lot. As long as you're sensible and careful you'll be fine!

Catch you in a while ... Crocodile!

Best wishes,

S.

strike a blow - help with the housework
mean as a cut snake - angry
go the knuckle - have a fight with
after dark - shark
sunnies - sunglasses
crook - sick
dunny - toilet
drongo - idiot

2 January

Dear sport,

Happy New Year! And how's you? I'm packin' me bags today cos tomorrow I'm off to Auntie Sue's place for the rest of the hollies! I'll be her junior jilleroo for three whole weeks! A jilleroo's a girl who goes to the outback to learn all about working on a sheep or cattle station (ranch). If I was a boy I'd be a junior jackeroo!

Sue's sheep station's near Thargomindah in Queensland. It's spread over 3,000 square kilometres. That's nothing though. One sheep station in Western Australia is so big that it covers an area the size of Belgium!

Sue's husband, my uncle Dave, got killed in a riding accident about four years ago, so nowadays Sue and my 19-year-old cousin, Dean, run the place with the help of their two stockmen. Doesn't seem many people to look after 12,000 woolly rocks, does it? Woolly rocks are what the outbackers call sheep! See why!

One third of Oz is used for grazing sheep. They're kept for their meat and their wool (and their brilliant sense of humour!). Along with gold, they were one of the things that first made money for Australia back in the nineteenth century. People say that Oz got by "on the sheep's back". In other words, by selling their wool to Britain. Nowadays there are more than 160 million sheep in Oz. Or, to put it another way, eight sheep for every human being! Let's hope they don't ever decide to turn vicious!

Auntie Sue's place is 96 clicks (60 miles) from the nearest supermarket and school! And her postie only comes once every two weeks (so you'll probably get my letters yonks after I've sent them!). When Dean was younger he did all his learning through the School of the Air. He got his

lessons over the radio on the kitchen table. Him and a load of other kids were each stuck in _their_ own bit of nowhere and were all taught by a chalkie

who was miles away! Fancy doing all those lessons and not being able to see the teacher or any of your mates!

Talk to you soon,

Sharon

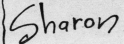

postie - postman

11 January

Hi mate!

Greetings from beyond the black stump! How d'ya like the pic? It's Auntie Sue's place out in the never never. Spot the neighbours!

It feels like I've been at Sue's for <u>ages</u> but this really is the first chance I've had to write you. It's shearing time right now so everyone on the station's going flat out like a lizard drinking! Including me! But I'm not whingeing. It's beaut' being a jilleroo. The best bit is tearing around on the quad bike helping muster up the woolly rocks for their yearly haircut.

Mustering's real hard yakka and by the end of the day I'm zonked! The moment my head touches the pillow I'm out like a light. No need for me to count sheep!

Once the sheep are mustered we take them into the big shed for clipping. Everyone works really hard and gets on really well. So I've made a load of new mates. Let me introduce you to some of them:

Inside the Shearing Shed.

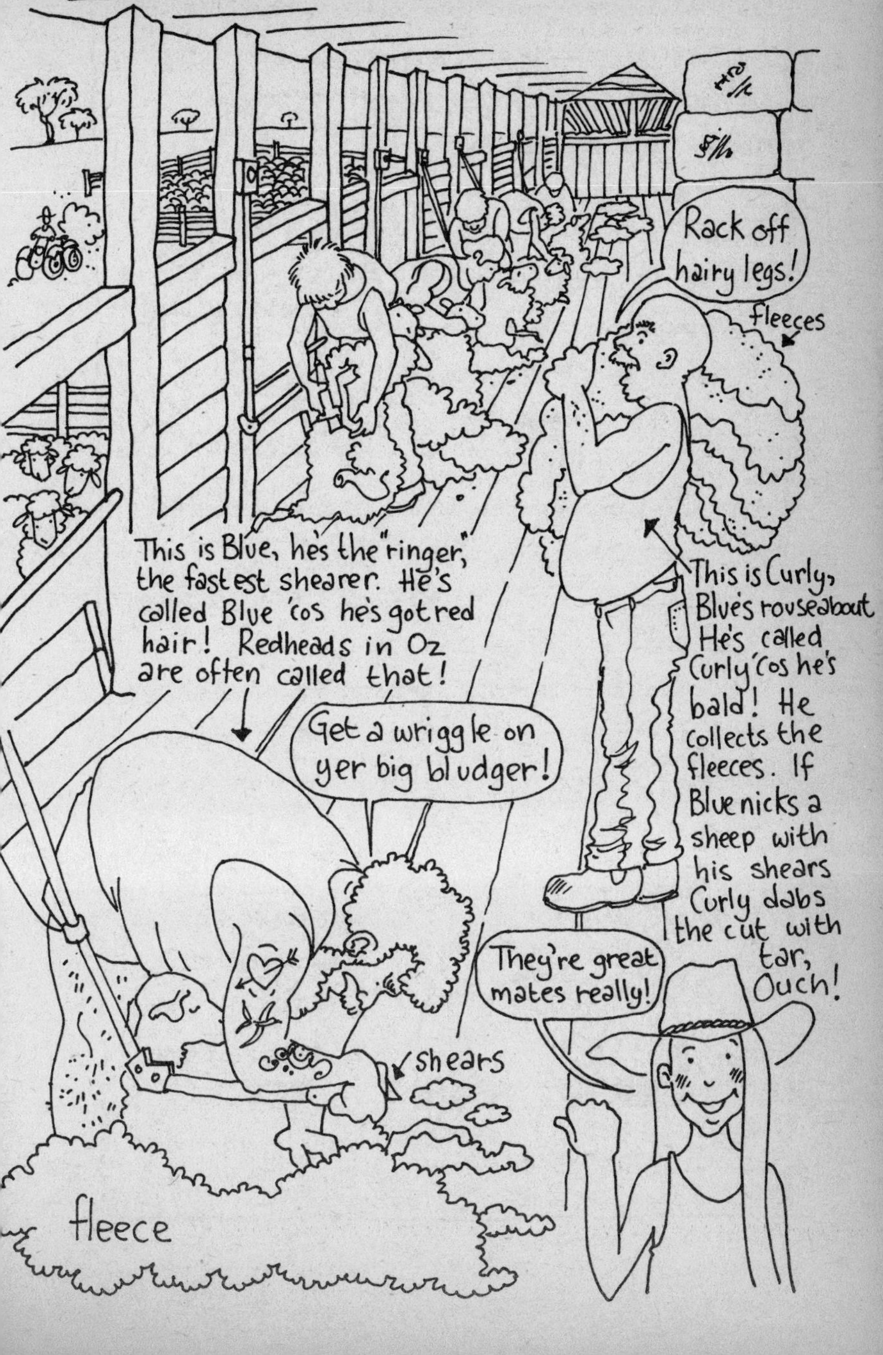

In the last ten days the shearers have whipped the fleeces off about 12,000 sheep! Some going, eh? Sometimes shearers have a race to see who can shear the most woolly rocks in a day! In 1892 a man set a record that still hasn't been broken - he did 321 in seven hours and 40 minutes. And that was just using hand

shears. Nowadays they all use electric clippers which are much faster and easier!

Since we finished shearing Jack's been showing me around the station and telling me loads of amazing stuff about the outback. He knows stacks! He's also asked if he can drop you a line and tell you something about Australian Aborigines. So watch out for his letter!

Jack grew up with Dean and did lots of his learning with him too. They both sat at the kitchen table listening to the trannie while ol' Eagle Eyes (Dean's governess) watched over them and made sure they didn't lark about or bludge off!

Right, that's all I can manage tonight. I'm completely zonked so I'm gonna crash out right now. Me and Jack are goin' walkabout in the bush in a few days so I need to build up my energy! More news from the bush telegraph soon!

All the best,

Shazza

flat out like a lizard drinking - working really hard

quad bike - motor bike with four wheels and big tyres

muster - round up

hard yakka - hard work

zonked - tired out

face fungus - beard

bludge - laze around

rouseabout - sheep shearer's helper

trannie - tranceiver (a two-way radio)

bush telegraph - way of passing info in the outback, usually by yapping

15 January

G'day pen-pal!

How's it going with you? It's roasting hot here right now and most of the time I've got a thirst you could photograph. S'right! Life's tough in the outback, especially for a city kid like me! But I'm <u>still</u> as happy as a dog with two tails and am having a great time!

I'm constantly being gobsmacked out by all the ace new things I'm seeing. Like the huge flock of blue and yellow and green budgies that suddenly <u>exploded</u> out of the trees when I opened the back door first thing this morning. There must have been <u>thousands</u> of them, all chirruping away and looking absolutely brilliant!

What a pity that some people like to keep 'em in cages!

The only thing I'm <u>not</u> keen on here are the <u>other</u> kind of budgies! They're the ones that Ozzies jokingly call dunny budgies. Yes, they're

flies! There's <u>squillions</u> of them and they drive you completely barmy. If you let 'em!

Maybe I should be wearing one of those hats you see Ozzies wearing in cartoons to keep all the dunny budgies and mozzies and blowies away!

G'day mate!

Then again ... perhaps not! Anyway, enough of that, it's time for my news!

Shearing's finished, so yesterday we all went out into the bush to have a celebration barbie. As we were collecting wood and stuff for the fire we surprised a whole mob of 'roos who'd been wetting their whistles at Sue's water hole. You should have seen them bound off into the night! They were awesome! I took this photo.

Things got even <u>more</u> awesome when their big male leader suddenly stopped and turned on Ned, who'd decided to chase them. Suddenly it was Ned who was being chased! Sue fired her shotgun in the air a couple of times and the 'roo took off after his mates, so Ned was saved. Later on Sue told me that a few years back one of her other dogs hadn't been quite so lucky. This time a 'roo had caught it and almost torn it in two with its big back claws. Yeah! As well as being amazing to see, 'roos can be amazingly nasty!

'Roos aren't the only sort of amazing animal we've got here on Oz. We've got absolutely tons more, as you'll probably know if you've ever looked at a book or a seen a film about our wildlife. The main reason we've got so many strange and awesome creatures here is because about 50 million years ago Oz broke away from the ginormous super-continent it had been attached to and began drifting north. After about 15 million years it arrived roughly where it is now (slow trip wasn't it!).

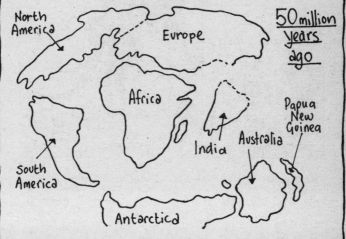

And all that time we were completely cut off from the rest of the world. As a result, our animals developed in their own sweet way. So we've ended up with stacks of wildlife that you won't find anywhere else on earth! Take a dekko at this bunch!

KANGAROOS ~ We've got more than 50 different sorts of 'roos! The smallest are only five centimetres tall but the biggest are more than two metres!

'Roos can't walk or run. They just <u>jump</u>! The best time to see 'roos in action is the evening and early morning. They spend the daytime snoozing in the shade.

Straight after they're born, the Joeys (baby 'roos), which are only about two-and-a-half centimetres long, have to drag themselves to their mum's pouch. They find their way there by following the pattern of the hairs on Ma's tum.

They stay in the pocket until they're eight months old but after that they nip out for a wander around, then eventually leave home for good.

Sometimes the Joeys aren't too keen on making their way in the big wide world. A 50 pound one was once seen <u>still</u> living in its mum's pocket! When Captain Cook heard the Aborigines calling these amazing beasts, "kangooroo", he wrote the name down ... and it's stuck ever since!

THE DUCK-BILLED PLATYPUS -

This is the Ozzy beast that gets everyone going cos it's a bit of everything. When some old-days Victorian scientists sent a dead one back from Oz to Pomland, their mates at the British Museum thought they were winding them up! They reckoned

they'd just stitched together various bits of
other animals for a laugh!

Here's the facts about them – and they are
the the <u>ridji didge</u>! The platypus lays eggs but
it's counted as a mammal because it suckles its
babies on milk when they eventually hatch out.*
It's got a furry body, webbed feet, a beaver's
tail and a duck's bill (but the duck says it wants
its bill back ... ha!). It spends half its time in
the water and half on land (like me!). It feeds
off the bottom of the stream but has to close
its eyes and ears when it's underwater (not like
me!). Its bill is electrosensitive so it knows when
it's getting near its nosh. Oh, and by the way,
the platypus is poisonous too! Hardly any
mammals are. The male has got a poisonous spur
(spike) on each of his back feet which he uses
to fight other males and to zap frogs with
(yeah, poor frogs!).

KOALAS ~

Everyone's favourite cuddly toy! Their name comes from the Aborigine word for "no drink" because they hardly ever drink. But, if you give one a friendly squeeze an' cuddle it'll more than likely pee all over you! They get their moisture from the eucalyptus leaves which they chew all day long!

They also get their dreamy look from the leaves because they contain a chemical that acts like a tranquilizer drug on the koalas. It sometimes makes them so dopey that they actually fall out of their trees (please, don't laugh!).

They've got no worries about being eaten by enemies because the eucalyptus gives the koalas a pong that other animals all find quite disgusting. Even fleas won't touch koalas! I don't want to upset you or anything but did you know that lots of stuffed toy koalas are made from kangaroo skins? It's sick isn't it?!

DINGO – These are wild dogs that live in the Outback. They were brought here from Asia thousands of years ago but some escaped into the wild and bred. Some Aborigines keep them as pets. One thing they use them for is keeping warm. The nights in the outback can get really cold. The aborigines call a freezing cold night a three-dog night. Because they need to snuggle up to at least three dingoes to stay warm!

Wild dingoes attack sheep. Just a few can kill a whole flock! A fence has been built to stop the dingoes of north-west Australia moving into south-east Australia. It's 5,531 kilometres (3,437 miles) from end to end and it's the longest in the world!

PLATYPUS FROG ~

Even though this is an amphibian its young develop in the mum's tum (rather than in eggs).

Then, when it's time for them to be born, she just sort of sicks them up! Happy birthday frogs!

Out to play children. I'm sick of you ... PUKE!

* By the way, in case you didn't know, a mammal's an animal that feeds its young with its own milk and gives birth to babies, not eggs (unless it happens to be a platypus, ha!). And an amphibian's an animal that lives on land, breeds in water and lays eggs (unless it happens to be a platypus frog!).

We've got stacks more weird and amazing animals

including a lizard that hasn't got any legs, a tortoise with a neck so long that it looks like a snake when its body's under the water and a bird called the Jesus bird which can walk on water! Well, it can't actually – it just looks like it can as it trots across the lily pads! I just haven't got the time and space to

Tortoise

Jesus bird

tell you about all the others. You'll just have to come Down Under and see them for yourself, won't you? So, get digging now!

Cop yer later!

Shazza

mozzies – mosquitoes

blowies – blowflies

dekko – look

ridji didge – the real thing

16 January

Hi mate!

I'm Jack. How're ya doin'? I'm writing to tell you a bit about Aboriginal people and our lives here in Oz. So, here goes...

   When the white settlers got to Oz there were probably about two-thirds of a million Aborigines living here. Most of the early settlers from Europe thought that the Aborigines were just a nuisance to be got rid of! Especially if they were living on good land.

It's our land now. Get lost.

   It was hard for the Aborigines to stick up for themselves. They were divided up into about 700

groups spread all over Australia, and they spoke about 250 different languages. (Even the two tribes who lived on opposite sides of Sydney Harbour didn't speak the same lingo!) So they couldn't even say,

We don't want these white folks here! Let's get together and kick 'em OUT!

?????

Huh?

And when Aborigines did defend themselves, they came off worse! Their spears were no match for the white blokes' guns.

Sometimes the settlers didn't need guns. Thousands of Aborigine people died from European diseases like smallpox and flu. And sometimes the whites just poisoned them. No wonder Aborigine people think the first white blokes who came here from Britain were <u>invaders</u> not settlers!

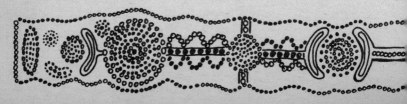

The whites thought that Australia wasn't owned by the Aborigines because they didn't put fences around it and farm it like people did back in Europe. But Aborigines don't see any need to fence the land. Our idea is that <u>we</u> belong to the land, rather than the land belonging to us! Those old-days Aborigines were really sensible and only took what they needed from nature. S'right mate! They were all ridji-didge conservationists!

Altogether, the Aborigines got a very bad deal from the white blokes! Most of them weren't allowed to vote in Australian elections until 1967! Nowadays, things are getting a bit better for

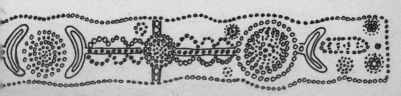

Aborigines. We're sticking up for ourselves at last and getting some land back from the government. White people who think that Aborigines got treated real bad are helping us to do this. Some Aborigines are writing books about our beliefs and way of life so that people understand us better. Other Aborigines have got really famous for their paintings which are now sold in art galleries all over the world.

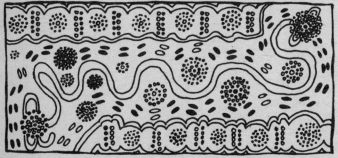

Lots of Aborigine paintings like this one are to do with our traditional beliefs about something called the Dreamtime. That's the time, a long, long, long while ago, when the world was first made. Aborigine people believe that animal-shaped spirits came from the sky and sea and

from underground. Then they travelled around Oz, creating all the trees and mountains and people and animals and things. All of these places are now very special to Aborigines and are known 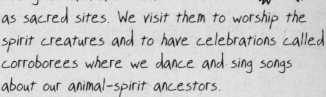 as sacred sites. We visit them to worship the spirit creatures and to have celebrations called corroborees where we dance and sing songs about our animal-spirit ancestors.

I've gotta rattle me dags! Me 'n' Dean have 60 metres of broken fence to mend this arvo! Now, what was that I was saying about Aborigines <u>not</u> fencing the land?

catch ya later,

Jack.

rattle me dags – get a move on

18 January

Coo-eee!

Hi mate. How're you doin'? It's Jack again. I'm
back, with letter number two! For starters here's
a Dreamtime story which will help you understand
some of our beliefs. I've made you some
traditional Aborigine pictures to go with it. Hope
you like 'em all.

The Hare-Wallaby people lived at Uluru. One
day they insulted the Mulga-Seed people who
lived nearby.

The Mulga-Seed people decided to get their revenge
on them by making a monster called Kulpunya.

Forked sticks for its ears

Mulga tree
branch for
its backbone

The
teeth of
a
marsupial
mole

bandicoot
tail

First they laid his skeleton out on the ground.

Then the medicine men sang him into being

As they chanted over the skeleton, evil went into it and it began to come alive.

Next morning the monster dingo was still **GROWING!**

The more they sang the more he grew.

The Mulga-Seed people sent Kulpunya to attack the Hare-Wallaby people.

111

Lunba the kingfisher woman gave the alarm but it was too late!

The Hare-Wallaby people were sleeping in the midday sun and taken unawares. Kulpunya caught them and destroyed most of them.

By the way, if you're ever lucky enough to visit Uluru, look out for the big rock called Mala. That's a Hare-Wallaby man who was turned to stone. The heap of boulders near the north face of Uluru are said to be scared Hare-Wallaby women running away from Kulpunya. The holes in the rock face are Kulpunya's footprints. All around the bottom of Uluru there are caves where animals like owls and rock wallabies (little kangaroos) live. The Pitjanjatjara Aborigine tribe paint their Dreamtime legends on the walls of these caves and hold their sacred ceremonies there.

OK! Now to a couple of other Aborigine things Shazza's asked me to tell you about. Didgeridoos and boomerangs! I'll start with didgeridoos. These long, hollow pipe instruments make a sort of droning sound and are played by Aborigine people at ceremonies, and for fun!

Didgeridoo

But they're not made by Aborigines. They're made by the insects known as termites.

When an Aborigine wants a new didgeridoo he cuts a nice straight branch from a gum tree then buries it in the termite mound, the huge earth hill where they live. The termites think the centre

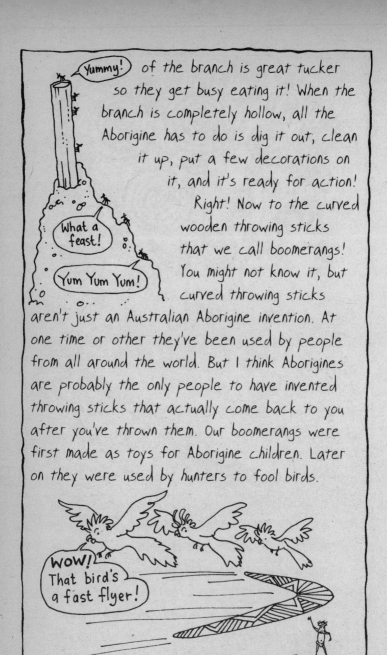

of the branch is great tucker so they get busy eating it! When the branch is completely hollow, all the Aborigine has to do is dig it out, clean it up, put a few decorations on it, and it's ready for action!

Right! Now to the curved wooden throwing sticks that we call boomerangs! You might not know it, but curved throwing sticks aren't just an Australian Aborigine invention. At one time or other they've been used by people from all around the world. But I think Aborigines are probably the only people to have invented throwing sticks that actually come back to you after you've thrown them. Our boomerangs were first made as toys for Aborigine children. Later on they were used by hunters to fool birds.

114

Not all boomerangs were thrown through the air. Some sort of cartwheeled along the ground and clobbered whatever animal the Aborigines happened to be hunting. If this is beginning to sound too bloodthirsty, don't worry. Boomerangs weren't just used as weapons! They were also used for digging, as a tool for levering and cutting, and as musical instruments – people bashed a couple of them together. Nowadays they're mainly used for sport and in Aboriginal ceremonies.

OK, that's it. It's been great talking to you. See yah!

Jack.

20 January

Hi there pen-pal!

Shazza here. How are you goin', mate? I hope
you enjoyed Jack's letters! I've only got a few
more days to go in the outback before I'm
winging my way back to Steak and Kidney. Then
it'll be time to go back to school. And that
means a new term and the end of my letter-
writing project to you. So I'll cut the cackle and
get a wriggle on!

 D'you believe in magic? Yesterday, I did, for a
moment or two! I was having a walkabout with
Jack, checking out the scene, when he picked
something off a clump of grass.

 "That's kerosene grass and this is its seed,"
he said, showing me a tiny
stem thing:

 "Wanna see a trick?"

 "Sure!" I said.

 Jack held the stem thing

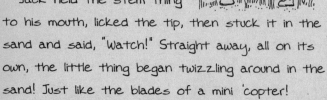

to his mouth, licked the tip, then stuck it in the
sand and said, "Watch!" Straight away, all on its
own, the little thing began twizzling around in the
sand! Just like the blades of a mini 'copter!

"Wow!" I yelled, "S'alive!"

"Course it is!" said Jack.

"But plants aren't supposed to do things like that," I said, still watching the thing. By now it had screwed itself nearly three centimetres into the sand!

"You try!" said Jack, and gave me a seed. So I did, and the same thing happened!

"Secret's in the strands," he said. He picked

another stem and pointed to the tip of the main bit of the seed which had three tiny threads wrapped around it. "Once they're wet, they unravel," he said. "That makes the fruit spin and drill itself into the sand. When d'you reckon that normally happens then?"

"Er ... when it rains?" I said.

"Yep!" he said. "The perfect time to plant seeds! For a plant that lives where it hardly ever rains, what could be better? It can plant itself just at the right time!"

We really have got some amazing plants and trees in Oz! I'll take you for a swift waltz around some of our most spectacular ones. Do you know any already? If I said to you, "Name me an Australian plant or tree!" I bet you'd say a gum. Three quarters of all Australian trees are gum trees. Their other name is eucalyptus. Maybe you've had eucalyptus when you've had a bad throat or cough? Not a whole tree though! Just a spoonful of the meddy! Their leaves contain a nice-smelling oil that is used in medicines and flavourings - even though it does make koalas smell bad to other animals!

Have you heard of a tea tree? It's not really a proper tea plant but this was the name Captain Cook's crew gave to it after they'd made a tea-coloured drink from its leaves. (They must have

been desperate for a "cuppa"!).
Its cool minty flavour and
smell are really trendy
nowadays and it's used in
shampoos and beauty packs
and stuff.

   I've left our most gross-looking tree, the boab,
until last. They've got huge grey trunks which
store water and sometimes measure more than 25
metres around! Pace it out and you'll see just how
big that is! When they lose their leaves in the
dry season we call them "the trees that god
planted upside down"!

   See what I mean? The most famous boab in
Oz is The Prison Tree at Wyndham in Western

Australia. It's so big and fat that its hollowed-out trunk was actually used to keep prisoners inside! Sometimes as many as 15!

Right, that's it for today, old flower. I'm off up a gum tree! Well, not really. I've actually got to start packing my stuff ready for my flight back to Steak and Kidney tomorrow. So your last bundle of chatter will be from good old Parramatta!

Catch you later,

S.

cut the cackle - stop yapping
get a riggle on - hurry up

24 January

Hi mate,

It's me, Shazza! I'm back in good old Steak and Kidney. Even though I had such a great time at Sue's, I'm really happy to be home again! Me and Kim spent two hours in our pool this arvo! It was cool (and wet!). The only thing that's making me feel a bit mis' is that this is my last ever letter to you. But don't worry, it's gonna be a good 'un!

While I was away Mum and Dad got a new car. I think Dad's fallen in love with it! He's out on our drive now, polishing away for all he's worth. (It wasn't even dirty!). I reckon he's showing off to the neighbours!

People are a bit like that in the big cities in Oz. Forever trying to impress everyone with what they've got! Does that sort of thing go on where you live? It's not a bit like that in the outback, though. I think everyone's too busy trying to survive!

Talking of the outback and surviving, my last few days there were really <u>brilliant</u>! Jack taught me some wicked Aborigine tricks for staying alive in the bush. I'm absolutely ... er ... "dying" (ha!) to tell you about them!

Remember how Burke and Wills, the explorers, came a cropper? Well, that was cos they didn't know how to get food from the wild, like Aborigines do. Aboriginal people have been living off the land for thousands of years so they're experts! The ones near the sea caught fish in traps made from stones and speared turtles from their canoes.

Some are even said to have used dolphins to help them herd fish! Ones living further inland caught snakes,

emus and kangaroos for their tucker. Quite a few still collect and eat traditional food like that nowadays.

Just in case you ever get stranded in the outback, I've made you this guide (with tons of help from Jack, of course!) on how to survive on tucker from the bush. Not big stuff (so you won't have to wrestle a 'roo!).
Imagine you're back o' beyond. Your Jeep has popped its tyres. You're waiting to be rescued. You could eat a horse and chase the jockey. And your

Biff boff!

throat's as dry as a Pommy's towel! But your food and water's gone! Waddya do? Just tuck in at Shazza & Jack's Outback Eatery. No worries!

Shazza & Jack's Bush Takeaway

Cyclorama Frog –

Whenever there's plenty of water around, this little bloke drinks until he's full to bursting,

then he burrows underground and waits for the next heavy rains to come! Sometimes for two years! Dig him up, give him a matey squeeze and he'll give you a matey drink in return!

Woollybutt grass - Pick off the seeds, take them out of their shells, grind them up between stones, mix them with water and bake them on a fire to make seed cake.

Damper - This is sometimes called swagman's bread or bush bread. You get a load of flour and mix it with water and salt, then bung the whole lot in a pan.

Put it in the hot coals of your fire and leave it until the dough's baked. It tastes ace - about 50 times better than the factory bread they sell in the supermarkets in Sydney!

Ooli worms - You'll find these in the rotting trunks of mangrove trees. Once you start pulling one out it'll keep coming and coming. They're about a foot long!

Sound like a bit of a yukky snack? No problem. Just pretend it's a monster helping of spaghetti blow-your-nose!

Yum!

Witchetty grubs-

These chubby little blokes are about as big as your finger. They live in bush roots and they're full of protein and fat. Roast them for a nice, peanutty flavour, or just eat them alive. But don't leave it too long or they'll turn into a moth and fly away. Ah ... lovely grub!

Honey ants -

These ants live underground and their tum is filled up with honey. It's about the size of a grape. Bite it off or just mix the whole ant with flour and water, then bake yourself some nice sweet honey damper.

Dilly bag -

If you're going shopping for bush tucker you'll need something to carry home all your goodies. Aborigines made themselves these naturally brilliant and brilliantly natural carry-alls out of woven tree bark.

Now, here's a nifty trick. To find out where bees kept their honey Aborigine people would sneak up on them then drop a bit of spider web on them (a bit like lassooing them, I guess!). When the bees flew away, they followed the unravelling web strands which led them to their nests!

Very Important Warning! You've really got to know what you're doing with bush tucker. So don't go trying to find this stuff on your own. You could end up with a belly ache, or <u>worse</u>! Take an expert with you. If you can't do that, you could always go to a posh restaurant in one of Oz's big cities where some have bush tucker on the menu.

~MENU~
Witchetty grub soup.
~
Cyclorama frog juice.
~
Ooli worm spaghetti.
~
Honey ant ice cream.

OK! That's it then. Me and Kim are off down the milk bar in a mo. We're gonna get ourselves a nice, icy cold, Banana Smoothie! It's an ace drink, made from milk and bananas. Or do you think we should just kiss a couple of those juicy frogs? Ha! So, it's finally time for me to say my last cheerio. And to say ta ta from Kim and Mum and Dad too. And "wuff wuff" from Dennis! It's been ripper writing to you. When I think of the fun I've had doing these letters it gives me an attack of warm fuzzies. That's Oz speak for feeling all cheerful and contented. Which reminds me! How's your Strine goin'? You reckon you could pass yourself off as a genuine Ozzie yet? If you ever do get to come to Oz look me up in Parramatta. I'll take you out to Manly and give you some surfing lessons. You'll be a rinky dink, ridji didge waxhead before you know it!

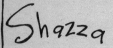

All the best to you pen-mate,

Shazza

PS If you hadn't already guessed, spaghetti blow-your-nose is our name for spaghetti bolognese. Ha ha! See ya!